Still Point

Poems and Meditations

Richard L. Graves

Copyright 2019

ALL RIGHTS RESERVED

No part of this work may be reproduced or transmitted in any form or by any means, whether electronic or mechanical, including photocopying and recording, or by any information storage or retrieval system without the proper written permission of the copyright owner.

1. Poetry. 2. Short Fiction. 3. Memoir

ISBN: 978-0-9980603-7-8

First Edition

10 9 8 7 6 5 4 3 2 1

For all the poets I have known, both written and unwritten,
who have taught and inspired me.

Except for the point, the still point, there would be no dance, and there is only the dance.

> T. S. Eliot

Contents

Remembering

Song for Lucille	1
The Morning Glory is a Weed	2
Don't Drink Out of the Dipper	3
Being Saved Every Day	4
Uncle George	5
Austin: August 1937	7
The Cottage	8
Going Home	9
Another Sunday	10
Mary	11
Olin Hill is Dead, Isn't He?	12
Southern Dialect	13
Rivers of Destiny: I Touch my Father's Face	14

Reflecting

Friendship	19
Gray Sky, Gray Sea	20
Smokey Shadows	21
Horn Island: Realization	23
Theology	24
The Leaves	25
Rain	26
Some Fruit	27
Pennies	28
Morning Walk along Jonathan Creek	29
The Tree of Life	30
Looking West across Tampa Bay	31
Nota Sonnet	32
Gray	33
Trains	34
They Come	35
Old Wood and Waltzes	36

Moth and Rust	37
Ars Poetica: The Muse	38
Words	39
Embers	40

Reconciling

Brother Maxey	43
The Lesson	45
The Oak Myself	46
Tremor	47
The Path	48
A Poem in Everyone	49
Some Rivers	50
The Way of Trees	51
River	52
Elvis	53
The Window	54
Acknowledgements	57
About the Author	59

REMEMBERING

Song for Lucille

This is a song for you, Mother.
You have been gone for so long
but still live in all that I do.
This is a song to celebrate your beauty,
raven hair and deep brown eyes,
and all that is good in you.
This is a song for you, Lucille.
Born at the summer solstice, you spread
joy and light wherever you went.
You loved those rocky hills; the mesquite
and cactus and scrubby cedar; the memory
of the Mescalero still lingering in the air;
the sleepy Colorado, rising in the hill
country, twisting its way to the Gulf,
giving life to all in its path.
You loved the poetry of that place
and passed that poetry on to me, not of that
place but that love, the eternal poem that
creates itself over and over and never dies.
This is a song for you, Lucille, lying so
still in that dry rocky land.

The Morning Glory is a Weed
In Memoriam: Lula Lee Burns Graves

Blue morning glories grow up the post of
the wooden front porch, wrapping their
arms around the post, reaching up almost
to the roof. Under the warm morning
sun, they open and bloom, sharing their
scant beauty with all who pass, stealing a
few moments of life from the dry land.
The morning glory is a weed.

Fugitive from the deep piney woods to the
east, she lives there with daughter and son-in-law.
Remembering, she takes up the hoe
each summer to tend tomatoes and squash,
weeding, watering, relishing each plant.
She works under the summer sun, singing,
*Sowing in the morning, sowing seeds of
kindness*, breathing heavily,
great beads forming on her brow, her long
cotton dress heavy with salty urine sweat.

Small house and garden plot on Sherman
Street, squeezed between railroad and
shop, warehouse and store. Fragile oasis
set against creeping industry.

In the evening she eats great slabs of pork,
real biscuits and gravy, string beans and
ham fat. She sleeps in peace and dreams of
ripening tomatoes and squash, of white-robed
angels playing harps that sound like banjos.

Don't Drink Out of the Dipper
A conversation in the kitchen, 1938

"Don't play with the Snows," my mother says.
"They're poor, and you know
their father's an alcoholic."

I listen and nod.
We don't make eye contact,
my mother and I.

"The Snows are poor,"
I tell myself.
"Their house is old
and all run down."

But Melba Snow. Melba Snow is . . .
> *smooth brown ankle and brown skin . . .*
> *soft brown hair and brown eyes . . .*
> *honey in her words . . . and I think*
> *of her mouth when she says . . .*

"Don't drink out of the dipper,"
my mother says.
"Those Snows are white trash. Don't
go to church. Don't have no clothes
to wear. Father drinks it all up. Stays
drunk all the time. Won't even work.
Live in that ugly green tar-paper house.
I feel so sorry for Mrs. Snow."

I listen to her words and say, "Yes'm,"
all the while thinking of Melba Snow's
smooth brown ankle and brown skin . . .

Being Saved Every Day

Mysticism is not first of all an act of union, but predominantly the life lived in the "knowledge" of this "wholly other" God.

Rudolf Otto, *Mysticism East and West*

Do you remember when you were a child in some country place far back in your life, a place that would embarrass your sophisticated now? Do you remember the day in your life, the time, the very moment when you were saved?

Do you remember the piano, all the earnest faces, the singing, the thunderous sincere sermons, but most of all do you remember you? The hollow feeling inside, the pounding heart, the taste of hot salty tears, the touching, the shaking hands, your own shaking body, empty now yet full to overflowing, then peace and silence and forgetfulness, like the calm after some wild summer storm.

It may surprise you to know that this is not a single event in your life but a permanent condition that gets into your blood, touching tissue and bone and every part of you, a condition you cannot escape.

You go about your daily life, eating and drinking, doing the laundry and making coffee, driving your car like any normal person, but all the while, under the surface, it's all there, like some dark subterranean river, crashing against the walls of your soul, coloring all you do.

How do you explain all this?

How do you explain the wind?
You only listen to it, feel it cold against your cheek,
watch it have its way with the morning sea.

Uncle George

I don't recall him saying a single word. He was a quiet man who left talking to women folk. He was slightly cross-eyed and always wore baggy khaki pants and shirt. He and his wife (my Aunt Hattie), their son George, Jr., and Hattie's mother ("Grannie" to all the grandchildren) lived in a small white cottage on the west side of Austin. In front of the house, across the street, was the municipal golf course. In back, down a rocky slope through scrubby mesquite and cedar trees, cactus and bull nettles, was the Colorado River.

Uncle George never had a regular job, even though he had a college degree and was qualified to manage a cotton compress. The problem, according to family tradition, was that the cotton compress was open only one month of the year, and for some reason Uncle George could never land a job that month. Consequently he spent his days—and sometimes nights—down at the river. He sold fishing gear and bait, rented boats, and served as a guide for novice fishermen. Aunt Hattie worked in a ladies' dress shop on Congress Avenue. On Sundays, rather than spend a nickel for bus fare, she walked some twenty blocks to the First Baptist Church downtown. Being thrifty, she eventually saved enough money to buy a fur coat which she wore on her Sunday jaunts. Family members would sell errant golf balls back to the golfers, which, along with Grannie's small pension, provided enough to scrape by, barely.

Uncle George's haven, the fish camp, was nothing more than a small clearing along the river bank. Several flat-bottomed boats were always pulled up along the muddy shore. A small storage shed at one side of the clearing held fishing gear and bait, empty drink bottles, and half-eaten sandwiches. In the center of the camp was a place for the nightly fire, cold embers testifying to the activity of the previous night.

Now, looking back on my childhood, I sometimes have a fantasy about Uncle George taking me with him down the rocky trail to the fish camp. I have wondered what it would be like to be out on the river at night, stars bright overhead, to sit around the camp fire, listening to the stories and tales of the fishermen. Perhaps I could have learned what it was that drew Uncle George to the river, day after day, throughout the year. Isolated from polite society and centered in a raw natural environment, the place contained—at least in my imagination—rich possibilities for the presence of myth. My guess is that the fishermen were not conscious of the mythic aspects of their lives and likely never talked about it. Perhaps they understood that merely talking about it would diminish the quality of it. The sacred can never be adequately expressed in words.

Austin: August, 1937

I remember, I remember.
A white frame cottage, there in a thicket of cedars
          near the muddy Colorado.

Inside: A wooden kitchen table. The oil cloth. Cornbread
          and goat's milk. The bed on the screened-in porch.
          The chair, with its chipped wooden arm. The worn
          linoleum, so cool to the feet.

Everywhere: The eternal sun, turning the skin golden
          brown. Dust and the pungent aroma of cedar
          and tobacco. The heat, so oppressive
          you can almost hear it.

Then at night: The banjo. The singing and laughter.
          Treat my daughter kindly. Say you'll do her no harm.
          If you will, I'll give to you my house and little barn,
          My horse, my cow, my sheep, my plow
          And my little farm . . .

But now: Only silence.
They sleep so still in the rocky land,
but some nights in the summer
when the moon is full and the air is rich with cedar,
I hear them once again, blending their voices with the cicada.
Then there is singing and laughter
and a certain fullness of the soul.

The Cottage

Fresh paint covers everything,
assaulting nostrils and lungs,
creating headaches and blurry throat,
this poison of breath and mind.

I come close now,
    cheek against the wall,
        close my eyes,
            listen.
Then with sharp blade begin
to scrape, gently, softly,
looking for tobacco and cedar,
old clothes, biscuits on cold
mornings, cornbread at noon,
all the residue of simple living.
    But also
the singing and laughter and voices.
Voices? Yes, can you hear them?
All there buried beneath the paint,
all longing to be free again.
    And I?
I am here to welcome them.

Going Home

Sitting there high on the crest of the hill,
    you see the lake below, the hills merging
        into the vortex, greens turning into
            gray and even darker gray.

You breathe, and the air you breathe
    feeds the memory.

Once more, in this stillness, their faces
    come alive, their voices, their spirits
        still living in this place.

This place, this rocky land, this mesquite and
    cedar and scrubby oak, this dry land
        where they too once drew breath.

Then you know they are still alive in you and
    you in them. And it comes to you above
        all else:

This is sacred ground.

Another Sunday

Another Sunday, years ago, I ran.
I ran, for running is a stay for grief.
And so I ran, whispering beneath my breath, "Why?"
but no answer came to me.
A gentle rain began to fall but still I ran.
Harder then the rain came down;
lightning hit the pines nearby.
And then it came to me:
This rain is God's own tears mingling with my own.
And so I ran til I could run no more.
I sat beneath a tree, in the gentle rain.

Mary

Almost five o'clock. I am in my
office, tired, ready to go home.
There in the open door stands Mary,
charming Mary, well-dressed Mary.
"What's up, Mary?"
"It's been a hard day. Really hard."
"Well, it's Martini time. Go on
home and have one for me."
Next day, out in a school somewhere,
visiting a teaching intern, a friend comes by:
"Did you know Mary took her life this morning?"
In shock and disbelief I weep, dry unbidden
tears from some unconscious spring.
Now, years later, I am weeping still.

Olin Hill is Dead, Isn't He?

You won't believe this, but I saw Olin Hill
last night, downtown, late, not many
folks around. He was walking back and
forth, back and forth. He looks just the
same as he always did, suit and tie,
tape measure still around his neck.

Remember? He had a men's clothing
store on College Street. You would go
in, pick out a suit, and he would take
the measurements. He would give it
to his wife, always behind the little white
curtain, running her sewing machine.
"Be ready in a week," he would say. Everyone
in town must have had a suit from Olin.

He kept asking me to take him home, but
I told him I don't know where home is.
Didn't make much sense. Said the sidewalk
is the only thing left, whatever that means.

If you want to try to see him, go downtown
late at night when nobody's around and the
moon is full or almost full. Be very still.
You might get a glimpse of him.

Southern Dialect

Whenever she speaks to the congregation
about the Women's Missionary Union,
I like to watch her mouth.
The words roll out
      round
          and
              smooth
and settle on the congregation like
      the scent of wild honeysuckle
          settles
              on the morning dew.
Her breasts move in rhythm with her words,
or is that my imagination?

Rivers of Destiny: I Touch My Father's Face

My father was a craftsman. As far back as I can remember, he had tools—saws, vises, planes, measuring tapes, a grinding stone, hammers and nails, as well as exotic tools, like large wooden pulleys and hemp rope. There was a musty smell in the dark corner of the garage, which was his kingdom. I remember him—a wiry man never weighing more than 150 pounds—carrying a square of shingles on his back up a ladder in the heat of summer. He was agile. He could balance easily in high places and never knew the name of fear. Once in the process of building our house, he and my brother and I lived in a garage he built. He even built the stove on which we cooked our meals. He could build anything that caught his imagination.

"Papa, it looks like you need a shave." The time is December, the place a hospital in Austin. He looks up in silence through his clear blue eyes, now so full of pain. He is perfectly lucid and recognizes me. His mind is as sharp as ever, but he can't breathe. The lead in paint has eaten into his lungs, and his heart has been weak since rheumatic fever in childhood. We all know the end is near.

I take up the electric razor. His skin is old and leathery, and he closes his eyes. His breathing is shallow and short. I touch his face with my hands.

Now, years later, I have some of his tools. Often I pick them up and hold them, look long into their shape, and touch the surfaces I have polished. I feel him around me everywhere.

And yet I grieve because I am not a craftsman. I constantly mis-measure simple tasks. When I use the saw, my lines are crooked. My nails bend before going all the way in. It's not that I don't try for I am my father's son. And so I keep trying, keep taking up his tools, keep wishing. That part of him that was determination is in me, too, but not the wisdom of his hands. I reach for it over and over, but it eludes me, and I grieve.

But in grief there is understanding. I am not a craftsman but something else. Some destiny beyond the father-son relationship forged my being. And today I drink from that destiny, an even larger force, and celebrate it. If I had been a craftsman, I would not have been a teacher. He wanted to be a teacher but couldn't so now he still lives in me—not just he, but something larger, too.

"My destiny is to be a teacher," a student once told me. And mine, too, I said to myself, remembering my father.

To fulfill that destiny is to be a builder, a builder of visions and dreams whose components are human rather than material. My tools are books and pen and paper. And yet there is something even beyond that—as though there were some grand architect inviting me to participate in some magnificent edifice, something beyond my wildest comprehension. My father was a practical man, not a visionary, but something calls me to a vision, a treasure, something sublime, something wild and wonderful beyond my fragile understanding.

I think I know what it is, this confluence of the rivers of destiny. I hear the voice of my father, but I hear the sound of the river, too. The sound is strong and full, and I know something good is there.

REFLECTING

Friendship

Who am I really? How can I get in touch with my real self, underlying all my surface behavior?

> Carl Rogers, *On Becoming a Person*

Words we say to describe ourselves,
but all the while, under the surface,
another is living there,
another more real than all the words
we say, another deeper than all
our masks and imitations.

Someday I may invite this stranger
in for all the world to see.
Someday—who knows?—we may
become the best of friends.

Gray Sky, Gray Sea

A distant mariner, washed ashore
on this vast infinity of wet gray sand,
I seek you out and find your face.
We walk hand in hand along the beach,
picking up gnarled driftwood,
caressing the ancient scars
worn smooth by ocean's touch.
At night we build a bonfire
and listen to the roiling sea.
We sing of Eros and wonder,
Is this bonfire just for us,
or is it a beacon for other mariners
lost on the cold night sea?

Smokey Shadows

If you would know anything
You must . . . touch the very peace
It issues from.

John Moffit

To know something, says John Moffit, you must know it not merely from the surface but from its very being, from its inner peace. Smokey Shadows Lodge is just the place for finding your inner peace. To get there, you travel to western North Carolina, to the heart of the Great Smoky Mountains. On the west side of Maggie Valley, you turn north off the main road and wind your way up the side of the mountain. At first the road is paved, narrow and rough but paved nevertheless. When it turns into gravel, you can hear rocks hitting the underside of your fenders. On these twisting, uncertain mountain roads, the best directions are "Follow the Signs."

The Lodge is old. Almost immediately you feel a kinship with the ancient timbers and stone. Soon you begin to breathe in rhythm with the place, slow and deliberate. There is not much talk. The atmosphere encourages silence. Words are soft, sometimes reduced to a whisper. The furniture is made from wood. The quilts are cotton and easy to touch. The food is mostly from local gardens.

On the back side of the Lodge is a porch that looks down the long valley to the west, hazy and gray in the late afternoon. Lush green mountains slope in from each side, converging at their base into Jonathan Creek, which flows down from Soco Gap and runs through the Valley. A few houses and a road are in the distance. Everything seems slow and very small. This perspective, almost hypnotic, calls the eye and the heart. You begin to find your place, your small place, in the vast wonder of creation. Away from the habits and demands and routines of life, you turn toward those elements that are so basic and fundamental—and so precious. The porch is like the entrance to some magnificent, natural cathedral, and the overwhelming impulse is one of awe and wonder. At Smokey Shadows you do not have to learn to mediate—it comes upon you, naturally and spontaneously.

The ultimate goal is to carry Smokey Shadows with us wherever we go. Obviously we cannot live at Smokey Shadows. Responsibility and work press in from many sides. In order to do the best possible work—and not burn out from exhaustion or boredom—we need an inner peace to guide us, keep us focused and protect us from distractions. Thus in the midst of busy, crowded days, we can turn aside and remember, "You don't have to go to Smokey Shadows to go to Smokey Shadows."

Horn Island: Realization

The celestial inverted cone of heaven, always there but needing to be realized.

Walter Anderson

In this stillness and solitude,
amid the sounds and rhythms of the natural world,
bird song, tree, wind and wave,
I come, step by step,
ever closer to the center.
Breath is slow.
Then with the warm Gulf at my ankles,
sand shifting beneath my feet,
rays of sunlight on my body,
I know.
I know and I know and I know.
I, a grain of sand in this infinite space,
for a single moment,
meld into the universe.

Theology

Theology is a game
      about
      God
      like
Monopoly is a game
      about
      money.
Having a theology
does not make you
      good
  any more than
winning in Monopoly
    makes you
      rich.

The Leaves

The wind bloweth where it listeth and you hear the sound of it, but you cannot tell where it is coming from or where it is going. So it is with everyone who is born of spirit.

John

New Year's Day and I rake the leaves.
The wind comes, scattering them
all in all directions.
Where is the formula to predict
where each will fall?
Where the theology to mend
my scattered soul?

What the wind says:

There is no theology
to mend your scattered soul.
Theology is just a prop to
support your personal opinions.
You put everything into pretty colored
boxes and put the boxes on a shelf.
Then you turn off the lights and
sleep your way through life.

No, there is no theology,
only surprise and mystery and wonder,
only the wind, the blessed ceaseless wind,
blowing where it listeth and
scattering our certainties in all directions.

Only the wind . . .

Rain

After the workshop,
on the way home,
rain fell in the mountains.

Some Fruit

Some fruit is not yet ripe,
but when ripeness comes
the taste is delicious.

Pennies

Finding a poem is like finding
a penny in the parking lot.
Pure luck? Maybe.
Or maybe it's because you're
looking down instead of looking
where you're going.

Once I found a dollar bill
by a pickup truck. Didn't
look for the owner. Just
stuck it in my pocket.

Morning Walk along Jonathan Creek

Morning, and I walk along the Creek,
waiting for a poem to come to me.
Ahead, the mountains, sun-dappled, silent.
Across the road, a field of corn, newly cut,
swarms of crows searching for breakfast
      in the warm earth.
Then the old house, shuttered and abandoned,
"No Trespassing" warning would-be intruders.
Now the Creek, running full, rocks splitting the
current, white and foaming, in the eddies
and bends field upon field of rocks.
Everywhere, the air fresh and cool, bringing
aromas from trees and weeds and flowering
plants, ever changing but never announcing
      their source.
I wait for a poem to come to me,
but the words will not say themselves.
And so I watch
      and listen
           and wonder,
abiding in this moment by the Creek.

The Tree of Life

The Psalms

See, there by the river is a tree,
a tree that brings forth its fruit in its own good season,
a tree whose leaf never withers but remains green and verdant,
a tree that prospers in all that it does.

Looking West across Tampa Bay

The finger that moves the Sun moves
us too. We come, strangers all, to this
place beside the Bay, this place where
earth and water meet. Some say it's
because we love the beer and seafood,
love to sing and dance. Yes, that's true,
but I say it's something more.
Tell me why it is, late afternoons,
we all turn and look west: to the town
far across the Bay, hazy now and faint;
the clouds, alive with shape and color;
the cargo ships, slow-moving like
the Sun itself; the Bay, brackish-gray,
dancing in rhythm with the wind.
We watch until the shadows linger and
darkness covers all. Then in the dark
we turn toward home, knowing west is
      home.

Nota Sonnet

The assignment is to write a sonnet fair.
A week we have to make it come to pass.
Six days fly by, no worry and no care.
Now here am I, the only dunce in class.

The topics all seem strange to me:
loss of love or loss of maiden fair,
loss of life or loss on raging sea.
The only loss I know is loss of hair.

I just can't sing this sonnet song,
a pitch too high and faulty rhyme,
my words askew and all gone wrong.
The meter's broke; I'm out of time.

In my poor pen no sonnet can I find.
Please help me finish this last line.

Gray

When December rains set in,
the whole world turns gray.
No more the palette of crimson
and gold and every shade of
green, nor the gentle tease of
autumn sun, nor the frantic search
for seeds and nuts and berries.
But do not despair, my friend,
for gray has a beauty of its own.
Gray is a stillness in the woods,
an uncertain step on slippery leaf,
a peace that summer sun can never
      comprehend.

Trains

Let's go find a train, you and I.
Do you hear it? Far away but
        not too far.

Let's go find the tracks:
        the sidings with their rusty rails and
          splintered ties and weeds growing up between the ties;
            the signal lights, stop and go and caution;
              the main line, seamless ribbon of steel
              stretching out forever.

Let's go find the station: the people coming
        and going, from where to where—Who knows?

Let's go find a train.
Let's go find a dream.

They Come

Sometimes in the evening
when the moon is high
and the wine is low in the glass,
they come,
rolling like distant thunder
on a warm summer night,
or ocean waves flinging their
foamy plume on some distant
shore, rolling, over and over,
in rhythm to some unheard music,
calling to the hunger of the soul.

Old Wood and Waltzes

Old wood's a memory
of trees young and green,
sunlight and springtime,
rich woodland supreme.

A waltz is a circle,
a moving circle of light,
turning and ever returning,
a moment of grace to delight.

Chorus:
Old wood and waltzes
make me feel blue.
Old wood and waltzes
always remind me of you.

Memories and circles
run through our days,
invisible angels
make sense of life's maze.

Memories and circles,
food for the soul,
caring and healing,
making us whole.

Chorus

Moth and Rust

Do you think it will last,
    this fashion,
        this trend,
            this fad?

You seem so confident,
    so self-assured,
        so certain.

But there is an ancient voice out there,
    an irresistible wind,
        a darkness on the horizon
            that sweeps everything away.

Even you and me.

Ars Poetica: The Muse

When she comes she comes.
I never know when or why.
I hear the knock, so faint.
My heart races; my mouth is dry.
I open the door and ask her in,
my words all jumbled.
I offer her a cup of coffee.
"Will you stay a while?"
"Just for a moment," she says.
I know she won't sleep with me.
Maybe just sit on the edge of
the couch and sip the coffee.

Words

The truth that can be told is not the eternal truth.

Lao-Tzu

You say that we need to talk.
What more can we say?
I see your face.
Gentle touch.
Breathless.
Enough.
.

Embers

Tell me how it is that
you measure an ember.
Is it by its heat, numeric values
in Fahrenheit or Centigrade?
Or by its length or breadth,
its shape in tiny cubic bits?
Or by the intensity of its
glow in light and color?
No, none of these will do.
The only true measure
is the measure of time,
in minutes or seconds or nanoseconds
but sometimes, sometimes even in years.

RECONCILING

Brother Maxey

My seventeen year old dogwood is dying. Last summer I did everything I could do to save it. I sprayed it with liquid chemicals, fertilized it, watered it, and pruned weeds from around the trunk. This past spring it was full of blooms, spectacular white to complement the azaleas. But now the leaves have turned spotted and wrinkled, then brown, and finally have dropped off. The limbs are weak and spongy, some almost bent to the ground. I wonder and hope. Will it make it through the winter and give us one more spectacular show of white next spring?

This is also what we said about Varner Maxey. "Yes, I know he is ill and very weak. He can hardly breathe, but maybe he will give us one more spectacular show." And he did, but he was so weak they had to lift him up on the stage. This was his last farewell. After that he went down fast, and he died in July.

Brother Maxey, as we called him, was a square dance caller. His voice was rich and guttural and full of Southern nuance. Sometimes it was loud and lusty, but then it would go down almost to a whisper. A few people said they could not understand him, but my contention was that the real dancers could. In my mind's eye I can see him now, standing up on the stage, microphone in hand, a twinkle of energy in his voice and eye. *One more couple down in the front. One more sexy good-looking couple; Yeah, here they come. Are you ready?*

Now the squares are full and Varner begins, music and voice blending into a hypnotic rhythm: *You star through . . . and pass through . . . and trade by . . . and slide through . . . now bend that line and star through in front of you.* Everything is a kaleidoscope of color. You touch a hand, pull by, touch another, turn, on and on, all in one beautiful, choreographed pattern. You hear the calls and respond at some deep visceral level beyond conscious awareness. The music becomes faster and faster, but—and this is important—it is never rushed. You breathe in rhythm to the calls and the music—and dance.

Once, years ago, later in the evening at a big dance, my partner and I found ourselves in a square with six really good dancers. The dance began, music, choreography, and rhythm blending into a whole. For a moment it seemed beyond time and space. The impulse was to close your eyes and become lost in the moment. But then the music stopped—the dance was over. We all looked at each other. We sensed that we had been in a special place.

With the Mevlevi dancers of the Sufi tradition, the word "turning" has sacred connotations. It signifies a moving meditation. Once when time had come for prayer, someone called out to the dancers to stop and come pray. Their response was, "We *are* praying." The word *dervish* means, literally, according to Coleman Barks, "doorway." Doorway to what, one might ask? For square dancers and Sufi dancers it is all the same. Square dancers' *circle left* is eerily similar to the Sufi moving meditation. The doorway is an opening, a path, if you will, to the still point, to "a spiritual remembering of the presence at the center of the universe."

The chapel was packed at the funeral. I had to stand in the back with some fifty other people. The organist played traditional music, but in my mind I was hearing Varner at his best. Had he planned his own funeral, it would likely have been a celebration. The music would have been festive, and all his friends would have been there.

Watching my dogwood this fall, I will think of Varner. I will be reminded that death is a natural part of the cycle of life. I will remember that after winter, spring will come once again. And I will remember to celebrate as often as possible. Not much time is left.

The Lesson

In memory of Andrew Jackson Graves, Southwest Texas State Teachers College, 1926

There on the rocky hill
where stands Old Main,
he came that summer morning
inquiring about work.
The president turned in his chair
and looked out the window.
"Do you see those Blacks out there,
building that sidewalk?
Every day after class
you can join them."
Now, years later, I his son
come to this place, this window,
these old yellow brick,
this sidewalk.
The trees are a silent witness
to it all, these trees
where he found respite
from the summer sun.
I touch their burly surface and listen.
What was the lesson
he learned that summer,
not in books but in pickax
and rock and concrete?
The trees whisper that truth to me
all over again, and I listen.
High on that rocky hill
I listen.

The Oak Myself

The wind, the sun and the sea
have left their marks on me.
Deep in the earth my roots go down,
anchoring, nurturing, sustaining me.

The wind, the sun and the sea
have left their marks on me.
Deep into God my roots go down,
anchoring, nurturing, sustaining me.

Tremor

[Satori] . . . is a kind of fiery baptism, and one has to go through the storm, the earthquake, the overthrowing of the mountains, and the breaking in pieces of the rocks . . . It is really another name for Enlightenment . . .

> D.T. Suzuki, *Essays in Zen Buddhism*

Just before lunch, outside by the
classroom door, she stood there,
weeping.

"What's wrong? Can I help?"
I feel her body tremble,
know the tears are real.

"No, I'm okay, really. I'm fine."
In a moment we each turn,
go our separate ways.

Then Saturday in the kitchen,
washing the morning dishes,
it came to me:

Somewhere, deep in the earth,
two massive plates of granite shift,
grinding their faces against each other,
sending shock waves to the surface,
convulsing all that's there.

Then all is quiet.
Peace and calm.
Sunrise, dew and dawn.
Warmth and breath and laughter.
It really is okay. It really is good.

The Path

To be spiritually minded is life and peace.

Romans

A spiritual path leads to the supreme
heights of mystical awareness:
peace that transcends all human understanding;
fullness, a sense of always having enough, no
matter how large or small that may be;
thanksgiving, seeing as gifts what others
may see as handicaps or burdens;
moments of incarnation, finding depth and
significance in ordinary events and experiences;
simplicity, knowing the purity of "uncluttered;"
intersections, chance meetings with others,
charged with a glow of depth and wisdom;
beauty, seeing grace not in the externals but
in line and flow beneath the surface;
and *miracles*, breathless moments of
insight in the dance of life, unexpected and
unexplained, but always as welcome as
gentle rain on the dry land.

A Poem in Everyone

In every person there is a story,
in every story a poem.

Some Rivers

Some rivers are inevitable,
like the morning sun or
mist in the winter woods,
coming unannounced but
coming just the same,
natural and easy,
familiar as morning slippers or
the shape of your own breath.
Watch the surface of the river,
feel the current with your hand,
but remember:
Some rivers—some rivers are inevitable.

The Way of Trees

I walk among the trees and
    feel their presence.
The way of trees is the way of roots,
    anchored in the earth,
drawing sustenance from rich,
    loamy soil.

The way of trees is the way of growth,
    green leaf, bud and flower,
        friend to butterfly, bird and bee.

The way of trees is the way of time
    and place,
embracing ineffable destiny
in rhythm to cricket song.

Root and bud and circle.
All tree. All mine.

River

There is a river flowing deep inside of me,
a river of pure spirit.
I don't know its source, when it began or where.
I remember it from childhood;
it seems to have been there forever.
Maybe it's a strand connecting me to the past,
shadowy faces, still voices, dark figures
     from long ago.

The river is deep and the current swift.
Sometimes it runs out of control, overflowing its banks.
Sometimes it goes underground, hidden from prying eyes.
But it's always there.
It runs through my waking hours and my dreams.
It is the best part of me.

Sometimes on this river of pure spirit
I float easily downstream,
buoyed up by the current.
I let go and it carries me along . . .
     let go . . .
          and let go . . .
               and flow with the current . . .

What is the River telling me?
Listen to the voice of the River:

Plunge into the depth of mystery.
Some people you love for a lifetime,
sacred beyond mortal or flesh,
sacred beyond sense and time,
eternally sacred, together as one.

Elvis

If you had seen him on the stage
at the end of his career,
you would say that he was bloated:
puffy cheeks and swollen eyes,
sweat dripping from his brow.
Just a ghost of the magic
that once was there.

We envied him so much, this king,
he who had everything:
golden voice of the gods,
energy and music in every move,
houses and land and wealth,
friends doting on his slightest wish,
women swarming in lines
just to touch his sequined shirt.

But the dark side:
beer and bourbon and pot;
pills to put you to sleep,
pills to keep you awake;
a raging restless unfilled hunger;
the real self having flown away
in some absent moment.

If I complain about my earthly plight,
brand this vision on my soul.
In my nothing there is no shade of night;
in my poverty keep me whole.

The Window

Abide in the calling wherein you are called and therein abide in God.

> Hindu proverb

Each morning when he comes down for breakfast, he
asks for a table by the window. The table is
small, only for two. White cloth, cloth napkin; fresh
cut flowers; good china and silver; the coffee, always
hot and fresh; orange juice, fresh-squeezed; eggs
cooked to order; thick-sliced bacon; homemade biscuits
       fresh from the oven.

But the window. The window looks out over Main
Street. Now in the early hours of morning the homeless
and addicts come and go, shabby, tired, restless,
walking slowly, as if having no purpose, just mindless
walking. He watches. He watches and remembers
another beggar from years ago deep in his past:

*Always in his wheelchair, Abraham has a regular place
on the sidewalk in front of Walgreens. He sells pencils,
five cents each. He is shabby and unshaven. His thick
glasses make his eyes look large. An old Army overcoat
hangs over his shoulders. He looks and smells like a beggar.*

*Each day he is in the same place, but on Saturday nights
he is at the Franklin Street Mission. A few others are also
there, mostly the homeless, drifters who have come to
Florida for the warm weather, a large woman with her child.
The pastor is an ex-hockey player from Canada. The guys
and I are there, too, helping out, speaking, offering support,
During all that time, Abraham never said a single word.*

*One Sunday morning the guys and I go to Abraham's apartment
to take him to Big Church. They go in to help him; I
stay in the car. Strangely, a bizarre thought crosses my*

mind. Why not perform a miracle and say "Abraham, come on down here?" I feel shame for harboring such a thought. Abraham is hopelessly handicapped, probably from birth, both mentally and physically.

All this was in his past. He had left Florida, become a teacher, then a faculty member in teacher education, a husband, a father, a citizen in his community. But then came the dream, the recurring dream that brought it all back to life:

The setting is springtime in Tampa, warm and sunny. I am wearing the white short-sleeved shirt with wine-colored figures, the shirt I found on my bunk, the shirt nobody claimed. I am walking along a four-lane drive with islands in the center, stately royal palms in the islands, much like the beautiful Bayshore Drive in Tampa. As I begin to cross the road, I see Abraham coming toward me. He is crossing, too, but going in the other direction. As we meet, he whispers in my ear, but the traffic is heavy and I cannot understand what he is telling me. Then he is pulled off into his infinity and I into mine.

"What is it that Abraham is trying to tell me?"
The message is so important yet so elusive.

He finishes his breakfast and looks at his watch. Almost time to go. Must be at the school by eight. Traffic is always heavy. Then he remembers the words of a colleague. "Why are you wasting time in public schools? You should be staying home and doing research, the only way to get a national reputation. If you want to get a raise, that's what you should be doing."

He stands up, picks up the check, and turns toward the cashier. Then in a moment, the words almost tumble out of his mouth. "What could be more important than helping young people learn how to express themselves in writing?" He takes a breath—and the first step toward a new day.

Abraham (seated) at the Franklin Street Mission.

Acknowledgements

"The Morning Glory is a Weed," *Southeastern Conference on English in the Two Year College*, vol. 21 (Spring 1998), p. 15.

"Austin: August 1937," *Fine Lines*, Fall, 1996.

"Horn Island: Realization," Southern Mississippi Writing Project, n.d.

"The Lesson," *Hillviews*, vol. 37, no. 2, Fall, Winter, 2007, p. 80.

"Some Rivers," *Teaching English in the Two Year College*, vol. 19. No. 4 (December 1992). Reprinted in *Fine Lines*, Summer, 1998, p. 46.

"The Way of Trees," Assembly for Expanded Perspectives on Learning Newsletter, vol. 3, no. 3, special edition, 1995, p. 1.

"Tremor," *Camaraderie*, Raymond, MS: Hinds Community College, 1992, p. 13.

About the Author

Dick Graves is a fifth-generation Texan and his wife Lois a native Floridian, but they have chosen to make their home in Alabama. They have three children: Rebecca Johnson, Atlanta, Georgia; Jeffrey Graves, Staunton, Virginia; and Kathryn Anne Booher, Auburn, Alabama. Professor Emeritus at Auburn University, Dick holds the B.A., Baylor; M.Ed., University of Florida; and Ph.D., Florida State.

His interest in poetry dates back to his high school years, emerged while a professor at Auburn, and came into full bloom later in his life. In this collection he explores a broad range of topics, examines insights from various perspectives, and finds some reconciliation for conflicting views. He hopes you enjoy the writing.

www.ingramcontent.com/pod-product-compliance
Lightning Source LLC
Chambersburg PA
CBHW070439010526
44118CB00014B/2118